HOW TO DRAW
ANIME

Learn to Draw Anime and Manga
- Step by Step Anime Drawing Book for Kids & Adults -

Aimi Aikawa

Thank you for getting our book!

If you enjoy using it and you found it useful in your journey
of learning to draw, we would greatly appreciate
your review on Amazon.

Just head on over to this book's Amazon page and click
"Write a customer review".

We read each and every one of them. Thanks!

CONTENTS

INTRODUCTION

When you hear the word "anime", what do you think of? Majority would probably think: Japanese cartoons, awesome characters, or even epic fight scenes and cute school girls falling in love.

Well, you are not wrong, since anime covers a wide range of genre and can depict any themes or stories.

Anime is from the shortened Romanized word "animeshon" which means animation in Japan. The Japanese use the word animation as a blanket term to identify all kinds of animated production. Anime was first used as commercial animations dating back from 1917, and as it continuously grew in popularity, it became more and more diverse and started broadcasting nationally in Japan, then internationally.

Anime is usually a combination of character design, cinematography, graphic arts, and sound design. These components all-together make up for a harmo-nized work of art.

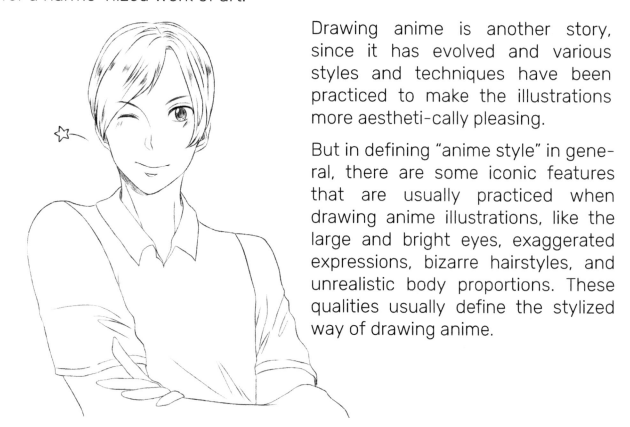

Drawing anime is another story, since it has evolved and various styles and techniques have been practiced to make the illustrations more aestheti-cally pleasing.

But in defining "anime style" in gene-ral, there are some iconic features that are usually practiced when drawing anime illustrations, like the large and bright eyes, exaggerated expressions, bizarre hairstyles, and unrealistic body proportions. These qualities usually define the stylized way of drawing anime.

Like any form of art, drawing anime requires you to start from the very basics. There are no shortcuts or magic when drawing. Even the greatest artists used to be frustrated in drawing an ill-proportioned body, so don't give up when you think you are not making any progress! It may be cliché to say over and over again but, practice does make perfect.

Your skills will not become professional overnight! Understanding every principle and guide and applying it is the way to make your drawing skills better each day. Another way of making better drawings is to always look for references, whether it is a pose for your character, or clothing designs, or even hairstyles!

Don't be afraid to utilize your re-sources around you. There is no harm done when you need to re-ference real-life objects to your anime illustrations, since in the first place, anime is a stylized version of the real world.

So, sharpen those pencils and prepare a lot of paper! Because in these how-to guides, we will dive into the colorful and crazy world of drawing anime!

DIFFERENCES IN ANIME HEAD SHAPES

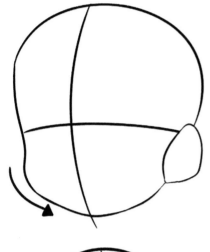

Drawing children's heads usually calls for rounder and softer features, especially the cheeks.

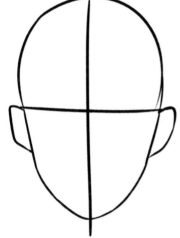

Masculine figures on the other hand tend to be longer and a lot sha rper than feminine ones.

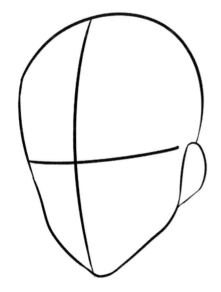

Older characters also have facial features that are more refined and sharper as compared to children.

Just remember that feminine figures are still more rounded compared to masculine ones which are sharper.

DRAWING AN ANIME HEAD
- FRONT VIEW -

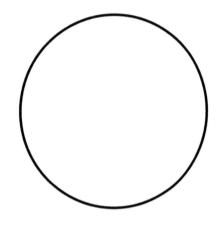

The basic shape that we need to draw an anime head is a circle!

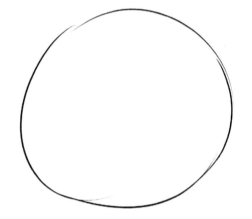

Drawing a perfect circle is not required. We can work with something like this one.

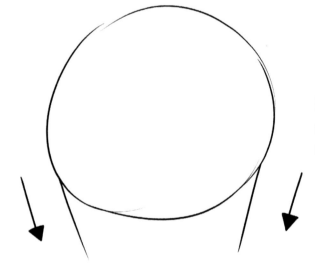

Draw two diagonal parallel lines downwards. These will be the cheeks of the head.

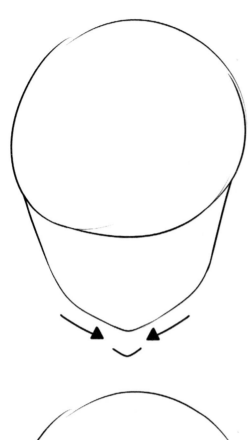

The jaw of the face would be two lines that meet in the center. the chin is shaped like a wide-open letter V.

Make sure that the edges where the cheek and the jaw meet and as well as the chin are not sharp.

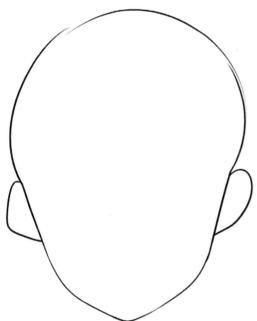

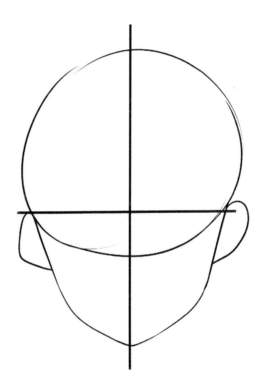

The head is now done! The next step would be
drawing the facial features.
A cross guideline placed in the middle of the face will help us know where
exactly to place the eyes, nose, and mouth.

DRAWING AN ANIME HEAD
- SIDE VIEW -

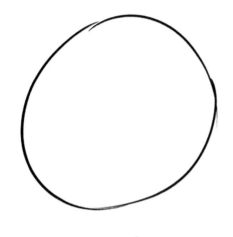

Like the front view, we will start with our trusty (imperfect) circle.

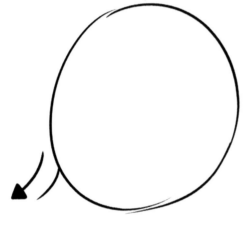

Draw a slightly curved line towards the direction where you want the head to face (in this example, left). This line is the bridge of the nose.

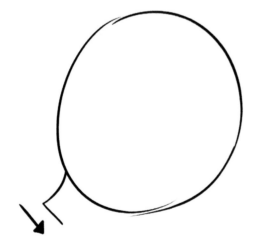

Then, draw another line from the bridge's tip going down straight.

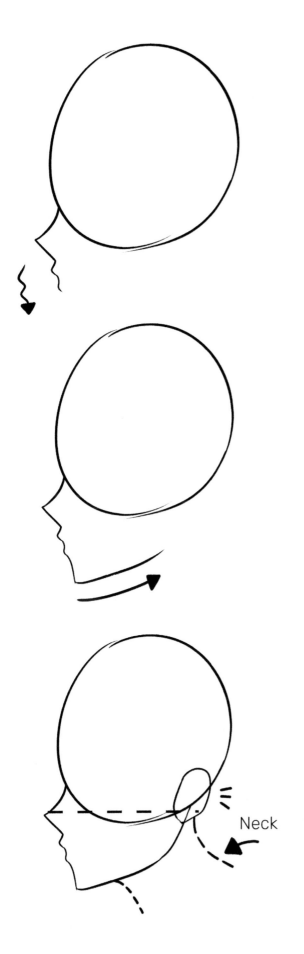

Then draw the lips by forming a wavy line downwards.

Draw the jaw line of the head by adding a line going up.

Continue to close the gap from the jawline with curved line going up. The ear is usually placed across the nose.

Neck

DRAWING AN ANIME HEAD
- 3/4 VIEW -

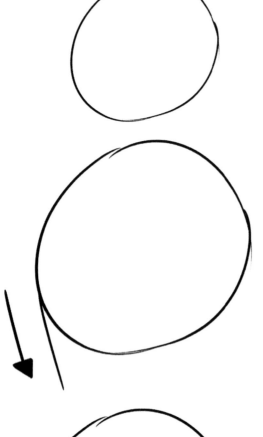

Like the front view, we will start with our trusty (imperfect) circle.

Draw a diagonal line downwards. This will be the left cheek.

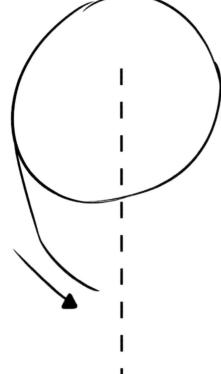

Draw the jaw by connecting a diagonal line from the tip of the cheek downwards.

Unlike in the front view, we will not draw it all the way until the center of the face.

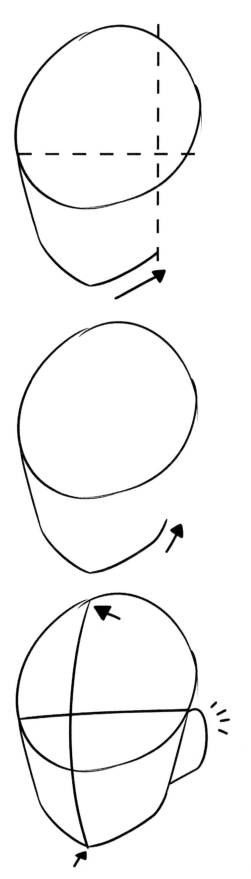

Draw another diagonal line, but this time upwards. Like the first jaw line, do not draw it all the way up. The chin is still shaped like a wide open letter V.

Connect a small line from the previous step going upwards. This is where the ear will be placed later.

Close the gap between the circle and the small line from the previous step. Add a guide for the ear and the cross guidelines for reference.

Remember that the vertical line of the cross guide still falls on the center of the face, in this case, from the top of the circle down to the chin.

BASIC ANIME EYES
– FRONT VIEW –

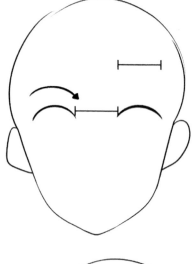

To start, draw two curved lines that are above the ears. The size of the curves will determine how wide the eyes will be.

Take note that the width between the eyes is around one eye length apart!

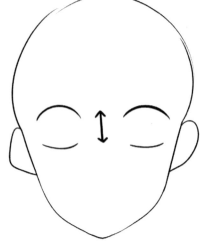

Next, draw another pair of curved lines facing upwards. These lines will determine the height of the eyes. You can adjust it according to your liking.

Add another pair of curved lines to each side. These will be the pupils of the eyes.

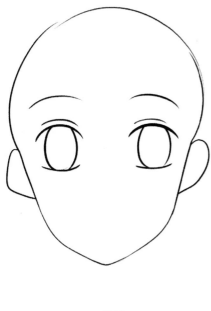

Add in other details to the eyes like the brows and lids which are placed right on top of the eyes.

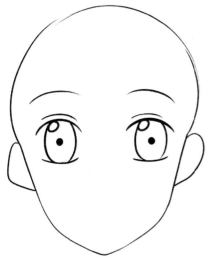

Lastly, add more life to the eyes by adding more details to them! You can add any shapes that you want to make your character more unique.

BASIC ANIME EYES
- SIDE VIEW -

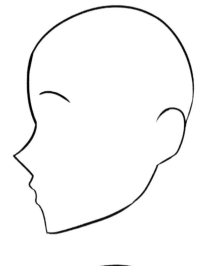

Drawing the side view eye follows the same process. We start with a curved line facing downwards.

But this time, we only drawone instead of drawing a pair since one side of the face is visibleif a character is facing sideways.

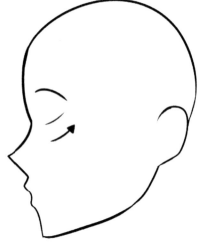

Draw another curved line below. It should face upwards but it must look a bit tilted as compared to the curved lines we draw on the front and 3/4 views.

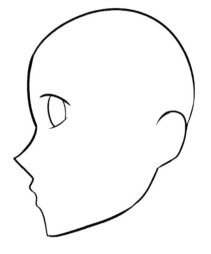

We will also add another set of curved lines inside of the first ones that we drew.

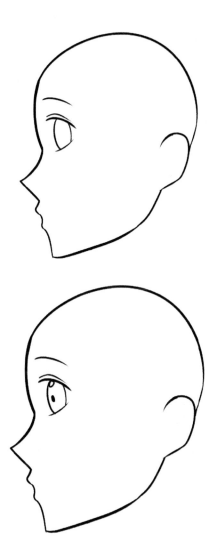

Don't forget the eyebrow and eyelid which are still placed on top of the eye.

Lastly, the details inside the eye.

BASIC ANIME EYES
- 3/4 VIEW -

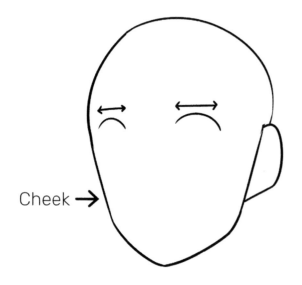

Cheek →

When drawing eyes in the 3/4 view, we start with the same pair of curved lines that face downwards, but this time, they do not have the same length.

The one that is beside the cheek will have a shorter length compared to the curved line beside the ear. The trick is that the shorter curve will have to be around 3/4 of the length of the other curved line!

We then add another pair of curved lines that are facing upward. They must be the same length as the first pair of curves we drew.

Like in the front view eyes, we add another pair of curved lines placed between the two pairs.

We will also add the eyebrows and the eyelids on top of the eyes.

Lastly, add the details inside the eyes.

STYLIZED ANIME EYES
- FEMININE EYES -

Now that we have covered the most basic steps in drawing anime eyes, we will now move forward into drawing more detailed and stylized eyes.

To give more depth and life to the eyes, instead of drawing a pair of curved lines we will draw two, and these two pairs will have to meet at the ends and form a banana like shape. Make sure to not make it very thick and wide.

Fill up the shape and add another pair of curved lines below, just like the basic anime eye shape tutorial.

In this example, the second pair of curved lines are a bit closer to the filled up shapes.

In drawing eyes, matured characters usually have a more narrow eye shape compared to young ones.

We will add another pair of curved lines inside just like the first tutorials that we had.

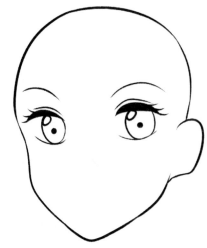

Then we add the lids, brows, eyelashes, and eye details.

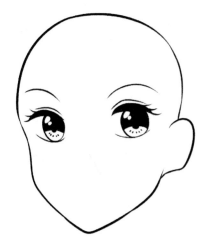

You can fill in the eyes if you want the character to have darker eyes.

Adding more shapes and details inside the eyes will make it look more alive and interesting!

STYLIZED ANIME EYES
- MASCULINE EYES -

Drawing masculine eyes follows the same procedure as basic eyes: we start with a pair of curved lines facing downwards.

Add little details at the end of each pair by drawing small angles going downwards.

You can also add these details to other eye styles that you want!

Draw the second pair of curved lines below. Masculine characters also tend to have more narrow eyes than feminine ones.

This time they do not have the same length as the first pair that we drew.

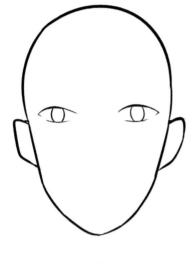

We will add another pair of curved lines inside just like the first tutorials that we had.

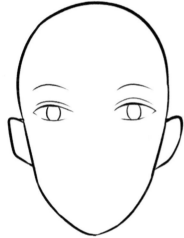

Add the eyelids and eyebrows.

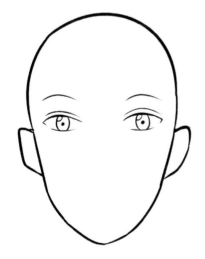

Lastly, add the details inside of the eyes like we always do.

You can fill the eyes up or add other shapes and details.

STYLIZED ANIME EYES
- ROUNDED EYES -

Rounded and big eyes are usually drawn for younger and brighter characters. We will start with the same shapes that we had when we started with the feminine styled eyes, but in this case make it more rounded like a crescent shape rather than a banana shape.

Draw the second pair of curved lines below. We want the eyes to be big and rounded, so leave a lot of space between the sets of curves.

Instead of drawing a pair of curved lines in between the first sets, we will draw a circles which touch that lower set of curves. This emphasizes the shape of the eyes that we want.

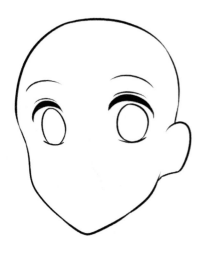

Add the eyelids and eyebrows on top of the eyes.

Lastly, add the details in the eyes.

Remember that this style can work with either feminine or masculine characters, the emphasis on this type of eyes is that the character would look younger and brighter!

STYLIZED ANIME EYES
- OTHER STYLE EXAMPLES -

Demon/Cat Eye

Lovely Eye

Matured
Feminine Eye

Dreamy Eye

Straight Eye

Sharp Masculine
Eye

Ringed Eye

Bored Eye

Pretty Eye

BASIC ANIME MOUTH

Anime mouth is pretty simple. Since the facial features are very stylized and simplified, most of the details of the mouth are not shown like shape of the lips.

When drawing the most basic forms of emotion, we will use various curved and straight lines. Take note of drawing a small line below to indicate the lower lip. Adding small lines at the edge of the mouth will also add the illusion of an upper and lower lip.

A smiling mouth is usually drawn with a curved facing upwards. Variations with the shape itself can denote the degree of "happiness" of the character. (more about expressions later!)

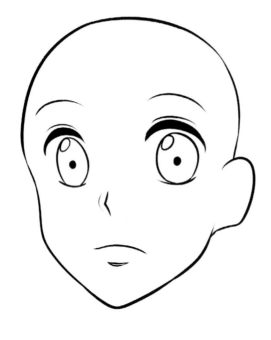

Frowning mouth on the other hand is drawn with a curve facing down. Like a smiling mouth, the difference in drawing the curve will affect the emotion of the character.

Like in this example, it looks more of a neutral expression rather than a sad one. (of course, the eyes and eyebrows add to the expression as well, like we saw in the previous tutorials!)

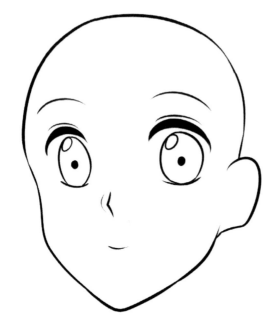

If you want to draw a little more details in the lips we can start with a little curve just below the nose. This will be the middle of the lips.

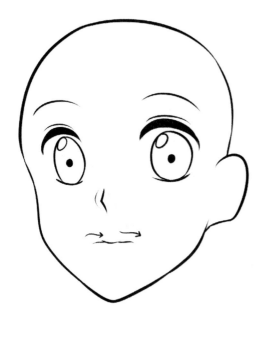

Add two curved lines beside the first one that we drew. You can make these two lines longer or shorter according to how long you want the lips to be.

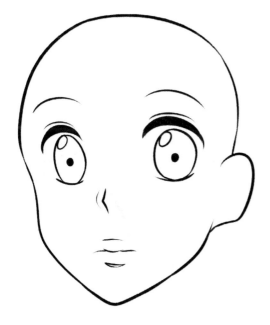

Add the line below that indicates the lower lip. Then add another above to indicate the upper lip. You can have thicker or thinner lips depending on how far from the mouth are the two lines.

BASIC ANIME EAR

To draw an anime ear, we start with a C-like shape followed by a curved line with a "bump".

Of course, you can adjust the shape of the ear according to your liking. Make it rounder, smaller, or even wider! Customizing the look of the ear will make your character look more unique.

Add a curved line facing downward on top of the lower part of the curve. This will be the lobe of the ear. This is usually where the earrings are placed.

Follow the shape of the main ear and trace a curve inside of it. Make sure that the curve will meet the lobe.

Close the space between the last curve and the lobe by drawing a wavy line. The little "bump" would be the tragus of the ear.

Add another curve inside the ear.

Add a curve beside the tragus of the ear. You can make this curve shorter or longer according to your liking.

Fill up the curve, this is the external ear canal, or the small opening in the ear. Add some more details and it's done!

BASIC ELF EAR

Drawing elf ears or fantasy ears has the same process as drawing normal shaped ears!

To start, draw a leaf like shape according to your liking. You can make it short or long, just remember to follow the basic shape of a leaf.

Add the tragus of the ear which is a curved line.

Follow the shape of the main ear and trace a curve inside of it.

Add the details inside of the ear including the external ear canal and you're done!

OTHER EAR STYLES

Stretched Lobe

Pierced Lobe

Small and Rounded
(younger characters)

Double Helix
Piercing

Short Elf Ear

Cat Ear
(usually animal ears
are placed on top of the
character's head)

DRAWING BASIC EMOTIONS

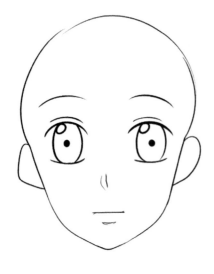

Expressions in anime drawings are usually seen through the eyebrows, eyes, and mouth. In this example, the face shows a neutral expression because of the facial features.

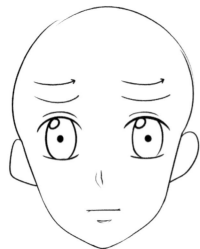

Changing the eyebrows to curves that face upwards will create a negative emotion. Even if the mouth has a neutral shape, we can see that the general emotion of the face changed.

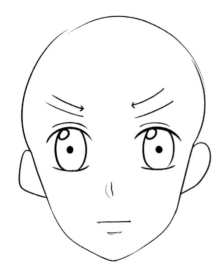

Drawing eyebrows that are going downwards that are slightly angled creates an angry face.

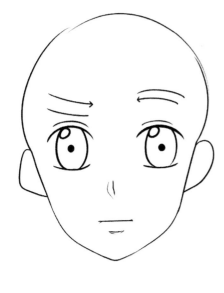

If we draw one eyebrow that is "sad" and another that is "angry", it will show a confused emotion.

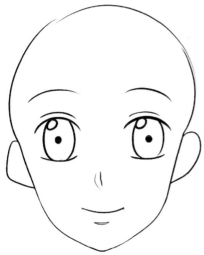

Changing the mouth shape will make the emotion stronger. In this example, we matched the neutral brow shape with a smiling mouth.

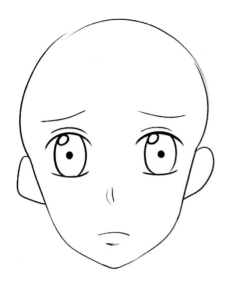

Make a sad expression by matching the sad brows with a frown. You can draw more intense emotions by making the features like the mouth more curved according to your liking.

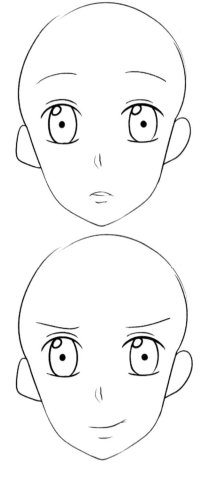

You can draw various mouth shapes to help convey a more interesting expression.

The key in drawing emotions is to mix and match the shapes of the facial features to create unique expressions for your drawing.

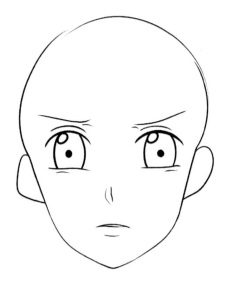

Changing the eye shape can also make a big difference in showing certain expressions.

Like in this example, the eyes are narrowed down and some lines around them are formed. One important tip to help you draw various expressions is to face a mirror and try to imitate the emotion that you want to have. Observe the general shape of your eyes, brows, and mouth. Then try to bring it into your character's face!

EXAGGERATED EXPRESSIONS

THESE EXPRESSIONS ARE USUALLY USED FOR COMEDIC RELIEF. THE FACIAL FEATURES ARE CARTOONIZED TO SHOW EXTREME EMOTIONS.

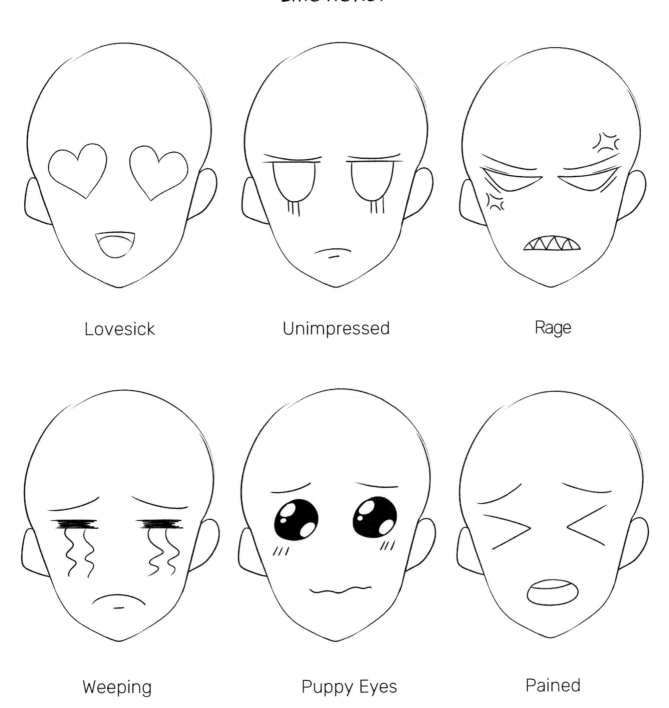

Lovesick

Unimpressed

Rage

Weeping

Puppy Eyes

Pained

DRAWING ANIME HAIR
- BASICS -

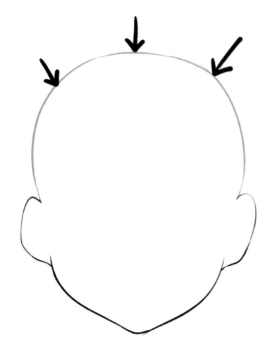

To start drawing hair, we must first think about where we want the partition or the division of the hair would be.

Usually it could start from the left, middle, or the right part of the head of the character. This will make it easier for us to draw the flow of the hair.

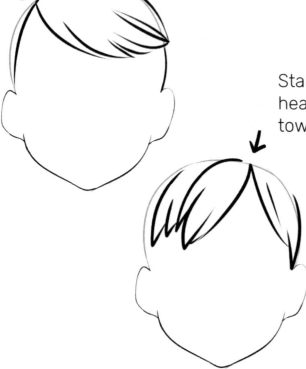

Starting the hair from the left side of the head will usually have bangs that flow towards the right side and vice versa.

While partition from the center of the head will usually result to bangs that are parted in the middle or full bangs.

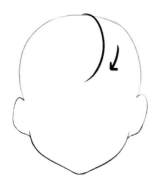

In this example, we will start with a division that is set on the middle of the head. Draw a curve downwards, the shape and length of the bangs will depend to your liking.

Next, draw another hair strand next to the first curve.

Close the gap between the first two hair strands by connecting a small curve starting from the end of the second strand towards the first.

It would be better if there is a small gap between the small curve and the first strand. It gives the illusion of a simplified "clump" of hair rather than drawing hair strands one by one.

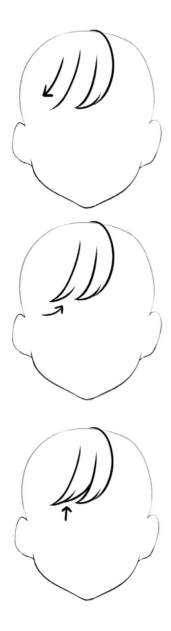

Repeat the process of creating another clump of air by drawing a strand, adding another beside it, then connecting the two by a much smaller curve between them.

You can also mix up the process instead of adding the small curve between the two strands, you can make the first two strands meet then connect the small curve to the first clump of hair.

Another variation you can do is to make two hair strands meet even without the help of a small curve.

Continue building up the bangs by mixing different ways of drawing clumps of hair.

The bangs usually stop before or upon reach the ears, in this case, the hair sections after the bangs are tucked behind the ear. You can make these sections longer if you prefer, some even cover up the ears. Drawing longer hair clump still follows the same steps when drawing bangs.

Trace the outline of the head to show the top of the hair.

Add the length of the hair using the same techniques when drawing the bangs. You can customize the length of the hair according to your liking.

For hair that is shorter and does not fall past the ears, remember to start where your original hair division was. This is where we will start the flow of the hair. (same thing applies to long hair)

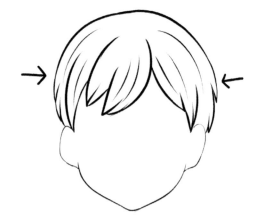

Add short hair strands before reaching the ears. In this example the hair looks choppy and spiky, you can always draw a different style of hair as you want.

DRAWING ANIME HAIR
- TYPES OF HAIR -

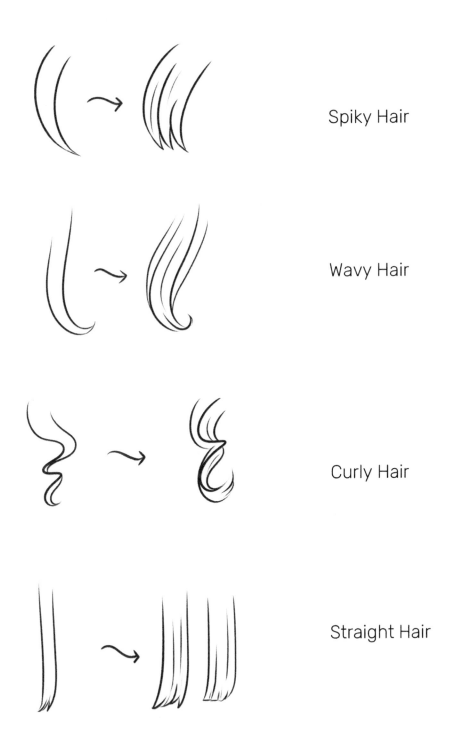

Spiky Hair

Wavy Hair

Curly Hair

Straight Hair

VARIOUS HAIRSTYLES

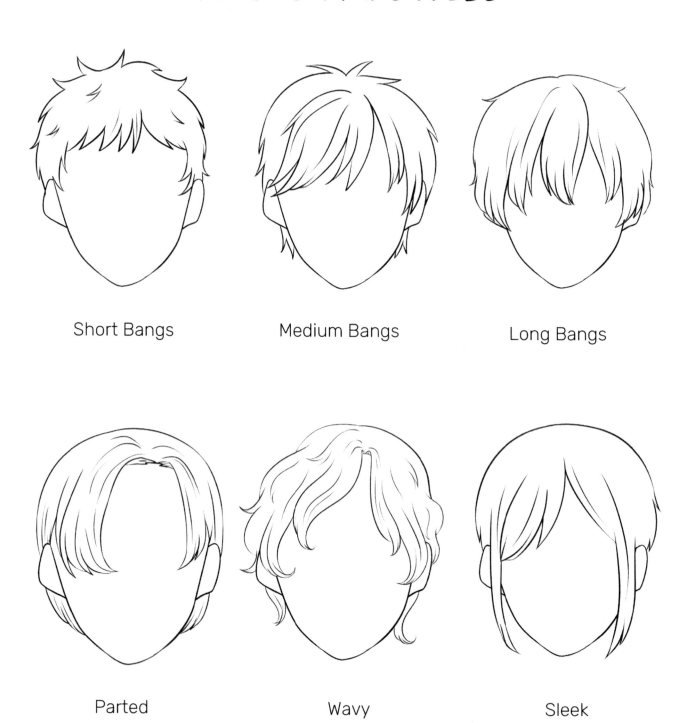

Short Bangs

Medium Bangs

Long Bangs

Parted

Wavy

Sleek

Apple

Bob

Half Updo

Low Ponytail

Twin Tails

One Side
Ponytail

Elegant Curls   Low Twin Tails   Princess Cut

Full Bangs   Twin Buns   Updo

SUMMARY AND IMPORTANT NOTES

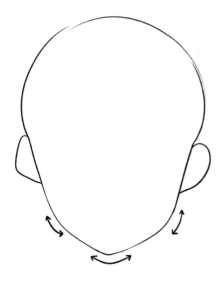

The edges of the face do not have sharp angles. They are drawn with rounded and smooth lines to make it more natural looking.

The width between the two eyes is around the width of an eye. The eyes are also in line with the ears.

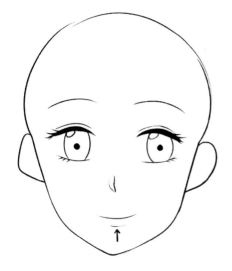

When drawing the mouth, a curve underneath it will make it look like the shape of the lip. This tip is applicable to all views of the head.

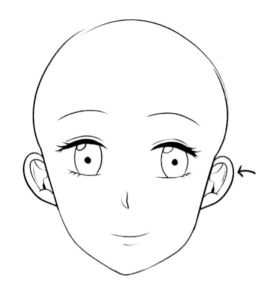

Don't forget the details of the ears!
Remember that ears still hold value in
making your character look unique!

Variation in drawing the strands of hair
will produce a more natural looking hair
for your character. Don't forget to add
some lines between the strands for
additional details in the hair.

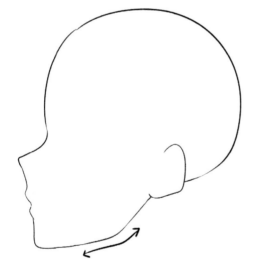

In drawing the side view, make sure to
draw the jaw line of the face as always,
all edges are drawn smoothly and
rounded.

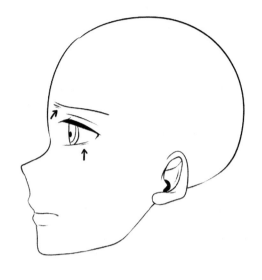

Mlake the expression more intense by adding lines along the brows and eyes to show the wrinkles the facial features make when showing a certain emotion.

Don't forget the variation that you can make with the eye shape and the details in it and the hairstyle.

Make the character a lot more interesting by mixing various facial features and styles!

The sky is the limit in drawing your character.

Don't be afraid to try a lot of styles to make your drawing look unique.

BASIC BODY PROPORTIONS

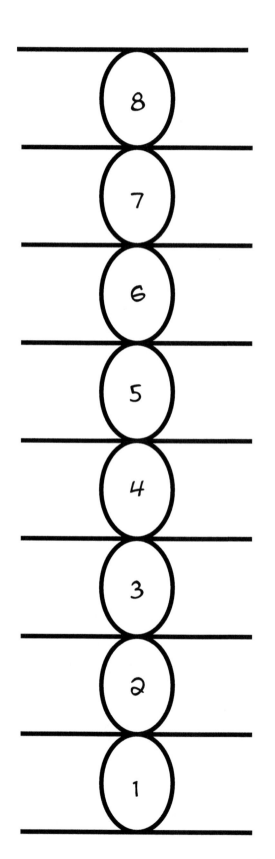

In drawing a full-body character, it is important to take note of the proportions of the body. Anime style is categorized as a stylized type of drawing, meaning, body parts and other features are heavily exaggerated.

But, even if it is expected that anime characters do not resemble realistic bodies and features, it doesn't mean that it won't follow the most basic rules of body proportions.

Principles and rules of drawing a well-proportioned body.

To start, we will use a "head" as a unit of measure in drawing the body. Normally, a human character is 8 heads tall, whether it is a feminine or masculine character.

It is important to use this technique as a beginner because it will help in identifying the proper places to put each and every body part.

The head itself would be on head 8 while the feet falls flat on head 1.

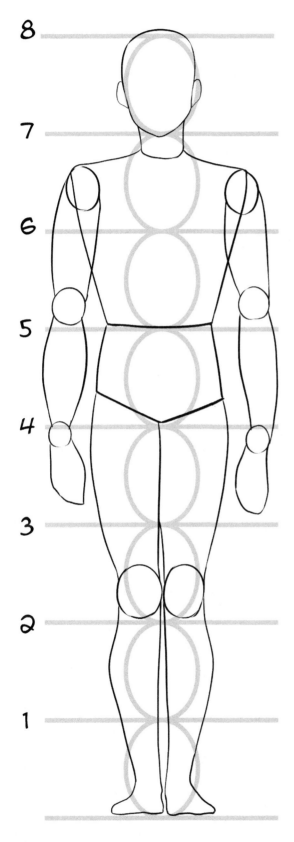

8- The head starts at 8 and the chin of the face ends in 7.

7- The neck starts in 7, shoulders are connected from the neck.

6- The middle point between the neck and the abdomen part of the body. This is where the chest lies.

5- The waist or the thinnest part of the torso is located here.

4- The crotch of the body is placed in the center of 4.

3- The end of the fingers are placed slightly above.

2- The bottom of the knees are placed in 2.

1- Halfway of the knees from the heels of the character.

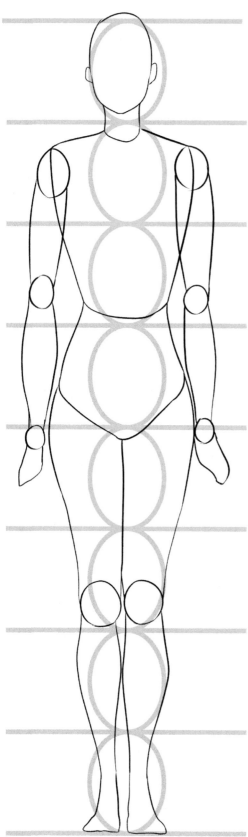

The same proportion principles are applied to a feminine figure.

Though, like all features of a more feminine character, shapes are more slender and narrower than a masculine character.

The usual parts that are noticeably slender are the shoulders, arms, legs, and the torso.

The waist is a lot thinner compared to the masculine body.

The hips (4) have the fullest shape.

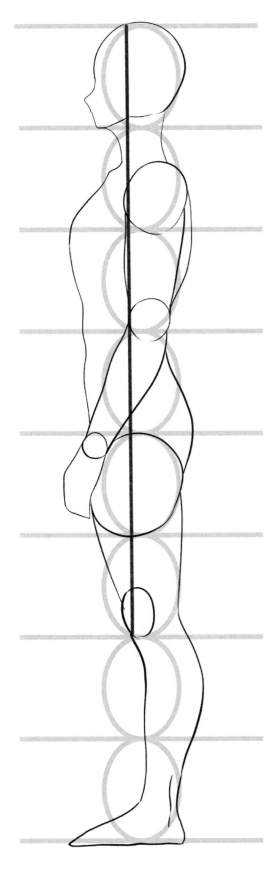

Drawing a side profile also follows the 8-heads proportion technique.

Drawing a line at the middle of the figure will further help in drawing the parts at the right position.

The chest, for either masculine or feminine figure, is not entirely flat when drawn in a side view.

The same goes for the stomach. Always remember that anime still follows the basic principles in drawing a human figure.

In this instance, a stomach or a chest cannot be entirely flat like a board since there are organs, muscles and bones inside the body.

The buttocks and calves are drawn on the other side of the middle line figure, while the chest and stomach are on the opposite.

DRAWING BASIC CLOTHES
- TOPS -

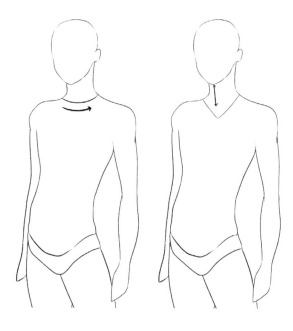

We will start with the most basic clothing piece which is a shirt. In this example, we have a lean and slender masculine figure as a model.

Start off with the neckline of the shirt. A curved line below the neck would be a crew-neck shirt. Of course, you can draw whatever neckline you want, like a V-neck, but remember that the middle of the "V" must align with the chin.

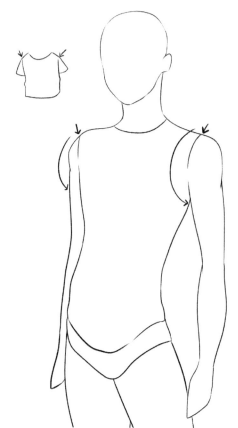

Then add the armholes, which are drawn as curved lines that loops around the arms. They usually rest on the shoulder blades.

But there are tops wherein the armholes are way past the shoulder blades, it all depends on the style of the clothing. but plain tops are usually designed like this.

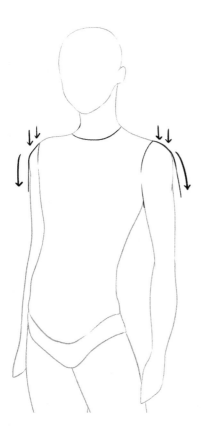

Add the sleeves by drawing curved lines that fall from the position of the shoulder blades downwards. Remember that even if the shirt is meant to be fitted or baggy, the key in drawing realistic flow of clothes is to imagine how gravity affects the cloth. In this example, the cloth will rest on top of the shoulder blades and flow freely beyond it.

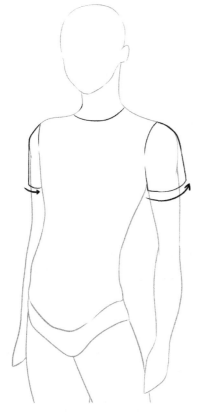

Connect the sleeves by drawing a curve between them. Make sure to make it a curved line to give it an illusion that the cloth is "wrapped" around the body.

Drawing a straight line will always result into an unnatural looking illustration!

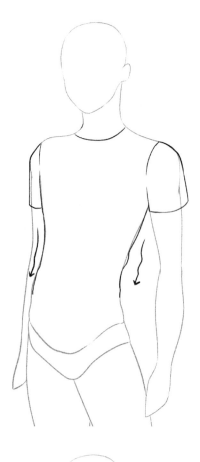

Draw the side seams of the shirt by adding two curved or wavy lines at each side of the torso.

These lines will give the illusion of folds or wrinkles in the cloth since our model is leaning a bit. Given that the body is not in a straight position, the clothes will also follow.

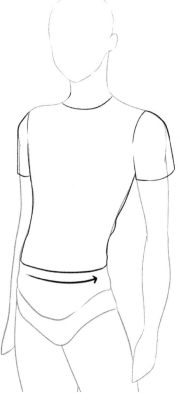

Draw the hem of the shirt like how the sleeves were drawn: curved line that looks like it was wrapped around the body. The length of the shirt will depend on your liking, you can make it short or long.

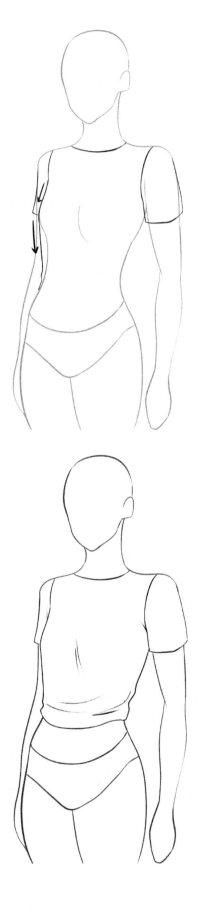

In drawing a shirt for a feminine figure, we follow the same steps, but there is a difference when we get to drawing the side seams.

Since feminine figures have busts, we will follow the technique with the sleeves of the shirt; the cloth will rest on the upper part of the bust and it will fall freely when it reaches down halfway.

In finishing a shirt for a feminine figure, make sure to add some folds at the bust area to indicate the presence of the chest.

Of course, if the bust size was drawn smaller, it only follows that there are smaller and shorter folds in this area.

DRAWING BASIC CLOTHES
- OUTERWEAR -

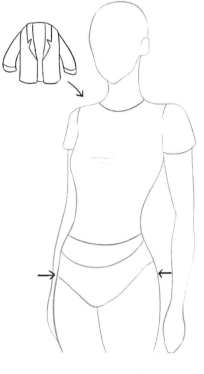

Outerwear includes jackets, coats, cardigans, sweaters, robes, and even blazers and hoodies. In this example, we will draw a blazer for this feminine figure that is wearing a simple undershirt.

First, determine the length of the outerwear. This will fall to your own preference; you can make it long like trench coats or short like cropped jackets.

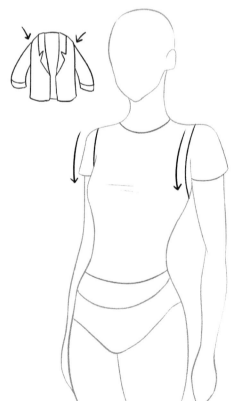

Like drawing shirts, make the arm hole of the blazer by drawing curved lines on top of the shirt's arm holes.

Remember that most outerwear are bigger than what the characters are wearing under. Make it fall a bit more than the shirt's armhole.

The next step is to draw the collar of the blazer. Put a gap between the neck and the collar itself.

Remember that outerwears are "resting" on top of the body. Make it look as if it is "wrapped" around the figure. Making it the same dimensions as the shirt will make it look flat and not layered.

Continue to draw the linings of the blazer as well as the lapels on the chest.

Draw the sleeves of the blazer. Make sure that it is larger than the shirt underneath to create an illusion of layered clothing.

Continue to connect the lapels with the hem of the blazer. Also remember that wearing outerwear will conceal most of the body shape of the figure. Like in this example, the chest area and the thin waist line of the figure will not be noticeable anymore.

The outerwear is now done! You can always experiment with the design, material, and type.

COMMON TOP STYLES

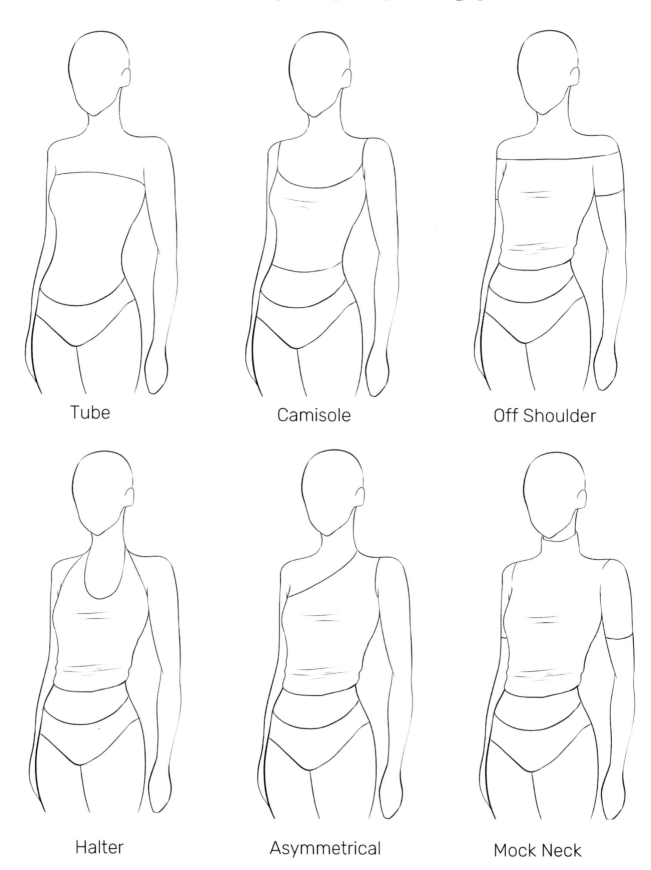

Tube

Camisole

Off Shoulder

Halter

Asymmetrical

Mock Neck

DIFFERENT KINDS OF SLEEVES

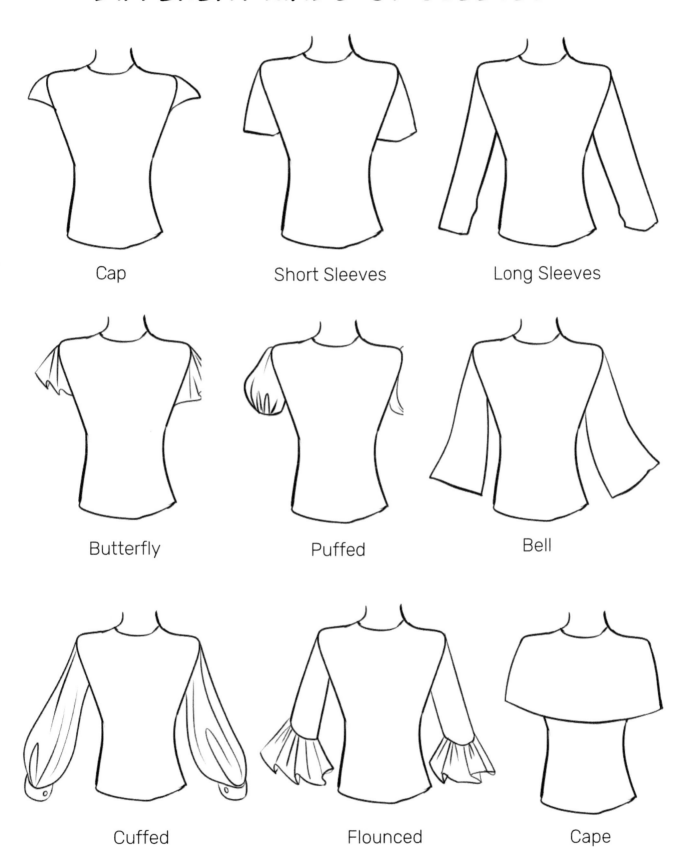

Cap

Short Sleeves

Long Sleeves

Butterfly

Puffed

Bell

Cuffed

Flounced

Cape

DIFFERENT KINDS OF COLLAR

Pointed Flat

Peter Pan

Cheasea

Notched

Mandarin

Shirt

Turtle Neck

Shawl

Tie

DRAWING BASIC CLOTHES
- BOTTOMS -

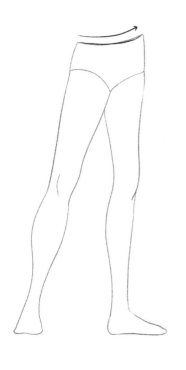

In this part, we will draw the most basic bottoms, which is a pair of pants. Start with the waist band of the pants by drawing a curved line along the waist of the body.

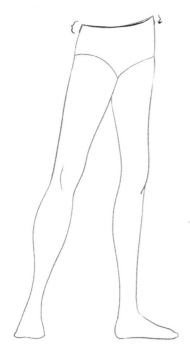

Decide on the width of the waist band, remember that this is where the belt loop will be placed later.

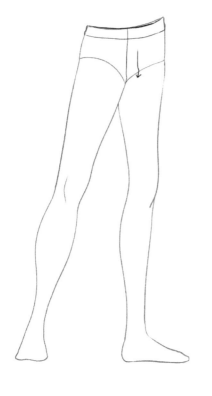

Draw a line at the middle of the pelvic area, this must past through the crotch of the body. This will be the crutch point of the pants.

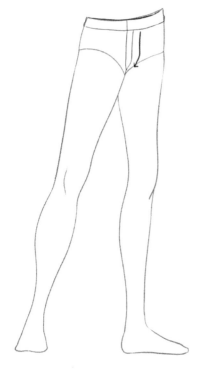

Add a curved line that will meet the crutch point, this line will be the fly of the pants where the zipper is usually located.

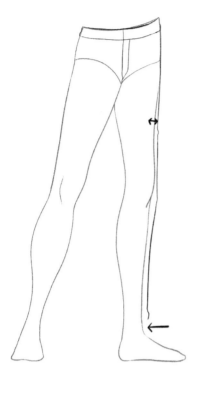

Determine the length of the pants, you can draw it shorter or longer according to your liking. Then draw the side seam from the waist band down to your preferred length. Remember that clothes have some gap between the skin itself and the cloth, except of course if the clothing was designed to be fitted or skin-tight.

Connect the side seams by drawing a curved line around the legs. This will be the leg opening of the pants.

Draw the finishing details such as the belt loops, pockets, and button. Add the folds in the crotch area. Remember that a resting position would have less folds than a dynamic one.

The same steps are used for shorts. The only difference is the length of the material itself. These steps are used for both feminine or masculine figures.

DRAWING BASIC CLOTHES
- BOTTOMS -

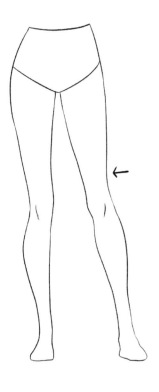

To start drawing a simple pencil skirt (straight cut), determine the length of the clothing. In this example, we will draw it a little above the knees.

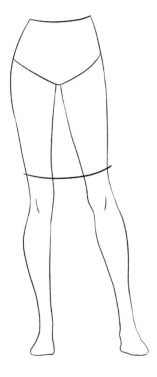

Draw a curved line across the legs. This will be the hem of the skirt.

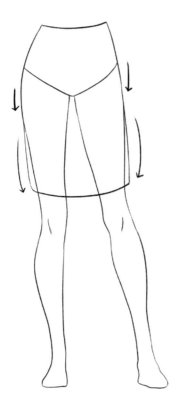

Connect the waist band and the hem by drawing the side seams using curved lines. Remember the technique where the cloth rests upon a body mass and falls freely after it. In this example, the cloth hugs the thighs that is why there are no gaps between the body and the cloth: after the thighs, the cloth falls down freely.

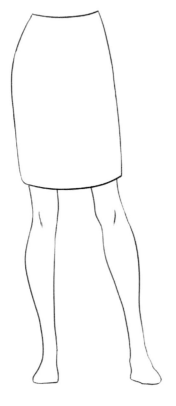

The simple pencil skirt is now done! You can add various details and designs to make it more unique.

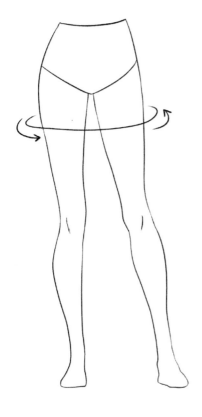

Another style of skirt that is typically seen wearing by anime characters is the pleated mini skirt. This type of skirt is usually worn by students or young women.

Start by determining the length that you want to have. In this example, the skirt rests around mid-thigh. Draw a curved line that looks like it is encircling the legs. This will provide a better guide to draw the clothing later.

Draw the side seams of the skirt and connect it to the hem's guide.

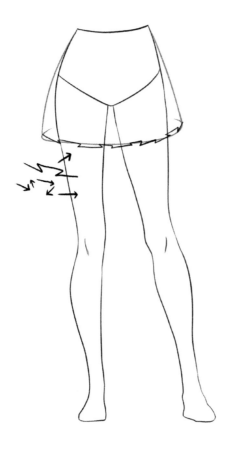

Start drawing zigzag patterns by the hem guide until it covers the whole length. You can make the lines wider or narrower, these lines will create the illusion of pleats within the skirt.

Connect the edges of the pleats to the waist band of the skirt. Do this to all the edges until you finish up all the pleats.

Connect the small folds of the pleats by adding small lines. This will give the illusion of folded and overlapping cloth.

The pleated skirt is now done! You can always change the length of the skirt and the width of the pleats' foldings according to your liking.

COMMON BOTTOM STYLES

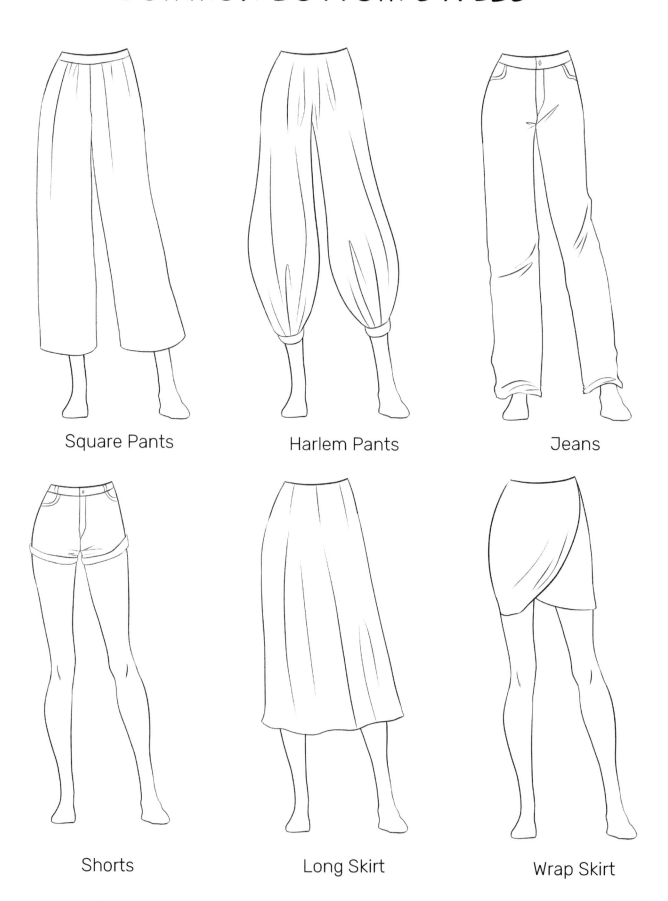

Square Pants

Harlem Pants

Jeans

Shorts

Long Skirt

Wrap Skirt

DRAWING BASIC CLOTHES
- HAT -

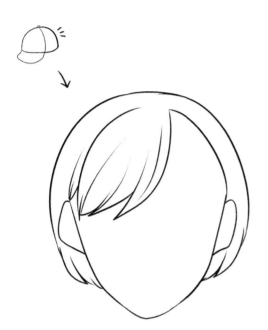

Drawing a hat is simple, all you have to remember is to follow the basic shape of the head. Also keep in mind that wearing a hat will tuck in the shape, so if a character's hair is fluffy or big, it will be mostly covered up by the hat.

In this example, we will be drawing a basic cap.

Start with the visor of the cap. The visor usually hides the forehead and the bangs of the head. Draw a curved line across the head of the character.

Complete the shape of the visor by drawing another curve below it.

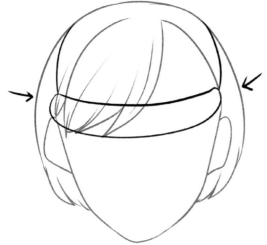

Add the panels of the cap. Remember that hats usually follow the shape of the head and not the hair, so in this example we draw two curved lines from the top of the head down to the edges of the visor following the real head shape of the character. The "extra" hair will be tucked inside of the hat so we will have to erase it later on.

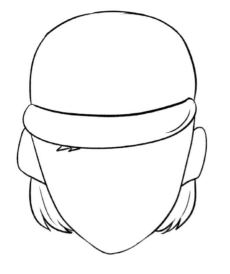

In the last step, we erase the "extra" hair that is supposed to be tucked inside of the hat as well as the bangs that are hidden inside of the visor.

OTHER HAT STYLES

Sun Hat
(Wide-brimmed)

Beanie

Witch's Hat

Cossack

Top Hat

Beret

COMMON HAIR ACCESSORIES

Ribbon

Bows

Hair Tie

Hair Band

Head Band

Hair Clips
and
Barrettes

DRAWING BASIC CLOTHES
- SHOES -

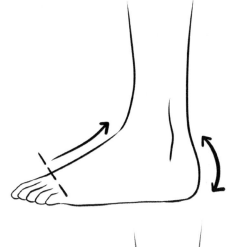

To start drawing a basic shoe, you need to understand the shape of a foot. Remember that the heel is curved, the toes are rounded, and there is a slope from the toes to the ankles.

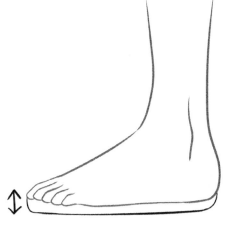

Determine the height you want your shoe to have. Remember that any type of shoe will always have a specific height, a shoe cannot be directly flat to the ground. For this example, we will use a normal height since we will be drawing a basic sneaker.

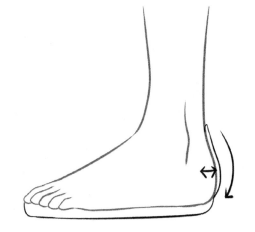

Add the back part of the shoe which houses the sole of the foot. Remember that it wraps around the foot itself so don't draw it flatly. Also put a small space between the foot and the shoe since a shoe does not fit like a glove or a sock.

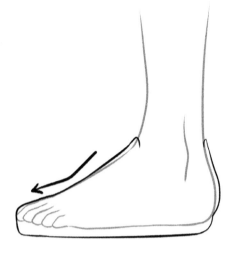

Add a sloped curve that connects the toes upwards. This would be the tongue of the shoe.

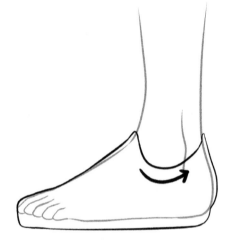

Add another curve from the tongue towards the sole of the shoe.

Add various details such as the shoe laces and seams. You can add any designs you want and experiment with the type of shoe you want your character to have.

OTHER SHOE STYLES

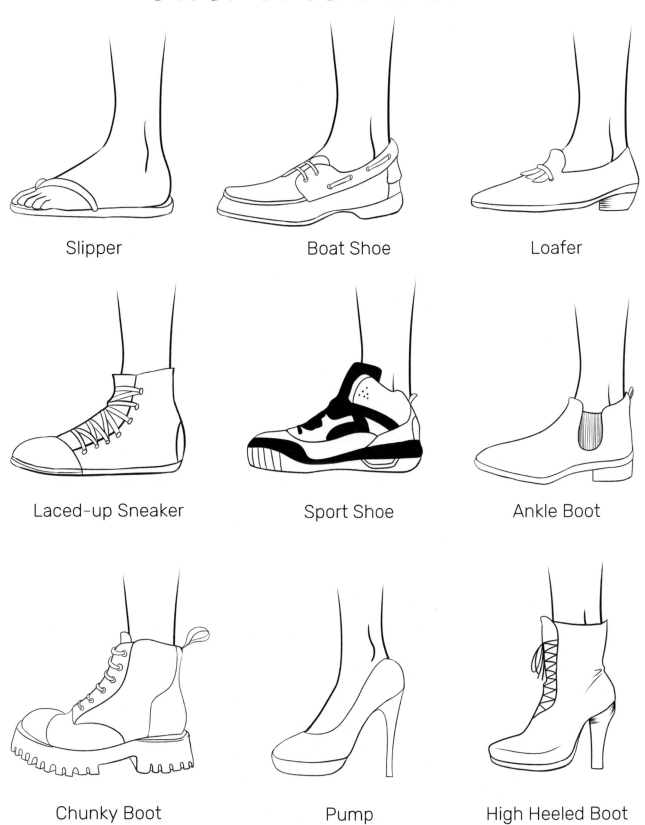

Slipper

Boat Shoe

Loafer

Laced-up Sneaker

Sport Shoe

Ankle Boot

Chunky Boot

Pump

High Heeled Boot

DRAWING BASIC CLOTHES
- SHOES WITH HEELS -

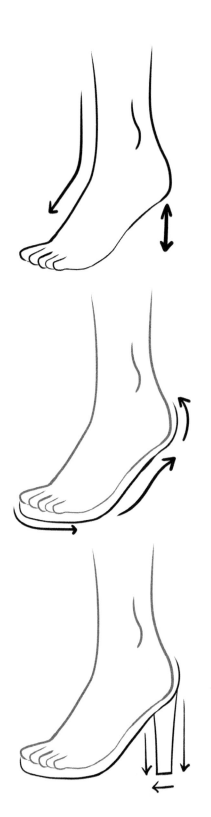

The process in drawing heeled shoes are almost the same in drawing low-heeled ones, the only difference is that the sole and slope is lifted higher. Start by determining the height of the heel. You can make it much higher or lower depending on the shoe that you want.

Like the second step in drawing low heeled shoes, draw the sole of the shoe and the rounded part at the back of the foot. Remember to leave a small gap between the actual foot and the shoe because shoes do not fit exactly like a glove.

Add the heel of the shoe. You can add different heel shape, like making it sharper, thicker, or even higher.

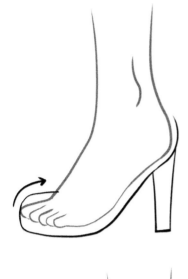

Add the toebox by drawing a curve line that outlines the toes.

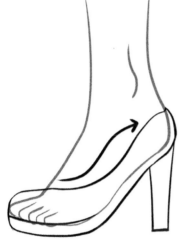

Draw the lining of the shoe by creating a curved line that connects the toebox and the sole of the shoe.

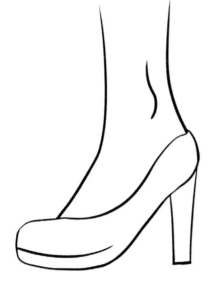

Finish off the shoe by adding various designs according to your liking.

DRAWING BASIC CHARACTERS
- YOUNG FEMALE -

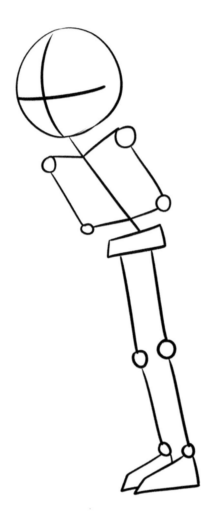

Now that we have covered the most basic tutorials, we can proceed in drawing the whole character itself!

In this example, we will draw a young female. We start by determining what pose she will have, remember to use basic shapes to build up the frame of the body: a circle for the head, lines for the limbs, circles for joints, and various polygons for the feet and the pelvic area.

Since we will draw a young girl, we can have her pose like this, which shows innocence and daintiness. Of course, you can have the character in any pose you prefer, but it would be better to show the character's personality through their pose.

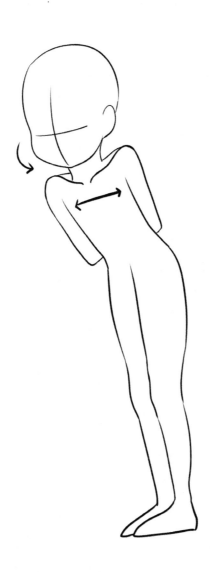

After drawing the basic frame, start defining the body shape of the character by outlining the basic shapes of the body.

Make sure to draw the face rounder especially around the cheeks. Doing this will make the character look more youthful. Also remember that children are a lot smaller than adults, so make their bodies thinner and shorter than the usual proportions.

Now we will start in drawing the face! Draw the face shape, eyes, brows, nose and mouth of the character. Since we are drawing a young character, make sure to make the eyes a bit bigger and rounder!

The personality of a character can also be seen in the eyes and the facial expression, so keep in mind of how you want your character to be seen! Are they the gentle type? The loud type? In this example, you can clearly see that the girl we are drawing is more of a shy and reserved character.

Draw the hair of the character according to your liking. Hairstyle can also speak about the personality of a character!

Remember the flow of the hair, like in this example, the pose of the character is slightly leaning to the side, that's why her hair falls to the side also.

Add various hair accessories like clips, bands, and hats to make your character more interesting!

Next thing to draw are the clothes! Look for various outfit inspirations for your character! You can look up the latest pieces in the internet or even from your own closet!

Also remember to match your character's outfit to their personality! A shy and reserved girl like her would mostly wear simple and feminine dresses.

Be aware of how the clothes will fall from the body. Like drawing the hair, make sure that you will show that the clothes will fall to the side if they are leaning to the side.

Add in other clothing accessories like the shoes and you're done! Drawing a young character in general focuses on having them look cute and active.

Add various accessories and make their hairstyles and clothes speak for their unique personalities!

DRAWING BASIC CHARACTERS
- YOUNG MALE -

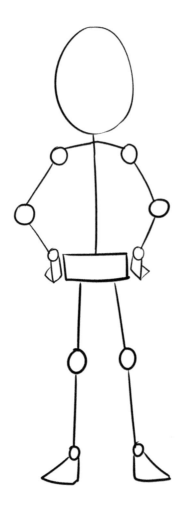

The next tutorials will follow the same steps as the young female tutorial, wherein the first thing to draw is the basic frame of the body which is composed of various shapes.

This character is also young, that's why we'll make the pose a bit cheeky and fun!

We will then proceed to the face of the character. Draw the face shape, eyes, ears, and mouth. A change in expression can make an interesting change in a character's personality.

Given that the character is young, a lively expression will match him well to show his personality well.

Add the hair to the head of the character. Since his design is more on the ac-tive side, a short and spiky hair style suits him well.

Add the clothes that will match your character. For this example, we will dress him fun clothes which young boys usually wear out. You can add more accessories or draw a variation of pieces and designs.

And now we're done! Always remember that you can always make your own variation in designing characters.

Just remember to follow the most basic guidelines and tips such as drawing young characters have rounder faces especially around the cheeks, bigger and rounder eyes, and thinner bodies.

DRAWING BASIC CHARACTERS
– MALE HIGH SCHOOL STUDENT –

The first step will also start with the basic framework of the body and a pose of the character.

High school students are often protagonists in many manga series, and drawing such is easy and follow the same procedures as drawing younger characters.

Since high school students are considered as "adults" in terms of body pro-portions, we will follow the standard in drawing the body of the character.

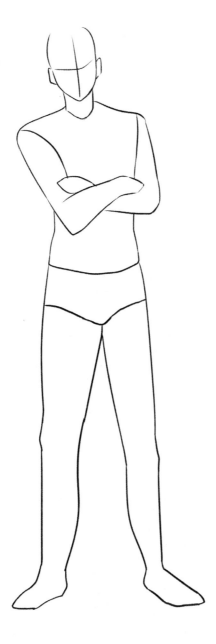

Follow the frame of the body by defining the body features such as the arms, torso, and legs.

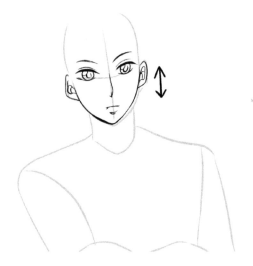

Start on adding details on the face of the character. Remember that these are older characters, so their facial features are a bit sharper and more refined than those of children.

Again, it can be helpful to know what type of character you are drawing beforehand so that you'll know what type of facial features will you draw to show their personality.

In this example, you can see that this guy is the serious type and a bit reserved, that's why their eye shape is a bit slender and their facial features are sharp.

Add the hair of your character, a variation in line thickness will make it less flat. Also take note of what hair style you are going for so that the hair strands are uniform together.

Next are the clothes! Drawing high school uniforms is fun! There are a lot of variations and accessories that you can add.

The standard Japanese uniform set is usually composed of a button up shirt (long sleeves, short sleeves during summer), an outerwear which is either a blazer or a cardigan, and trousers or skirts. For footwear, students either wear sneakers or loafers outside, and when inside their schools they switch to indoor shoes which look like soft loafers. Accessories usually vary, you can add ribbons and ties, or even plaid patterns to their skirts and trousers.

For this example, this cool guy is designed with the standard uniform set and sneakers, minus the neck tie.

And now we're done with our male high school student!

Remember to incorporate your character's personality in their clothes and expressions as well as their pose. These completes the drawing and makes it more alive.

DRAWING BASIC CHARACTERS
- FEMALE HIGH SCHOOL STUDENT -

The first step will also start with the basic framework of the body and a pose of the character.

With the framework, you can visualize how the character will look at the end.

Draw the face with the eyes, mouth, and brows. Never forget to be mindful of their expression.

Then, draw hair that matches our character's personality. Add her neck as well.

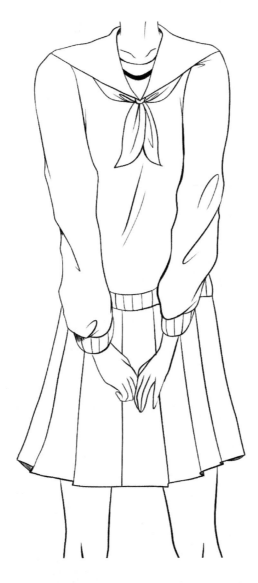

The next step is to draw the uniform. This type of uniform shown is another common uniform set students from Japan wear. it is called a "sailor FUKU" or simply sailor uniform.

Female students usually wear it with a bandanna tied around their necks, though ribbons and ties may also be used. Variation of outer wear is also common, like in the drawing, she is wearing a sweater outside of her sailor fuku. The uniform is also paired with a pleated skirt as bottoms.

Finish off the drawing by adding the shoes and other accessories. Like what was mentioned in drawing male high school students, loafers or sneakers can be worn by both girls and boys.

Socks are also an important accessory for uniform sets. Girls usually wear a variation of socks, some wear stockings, thigh-high socks, and like in this example, high socks that go with their shoes.

DRAWING BASIC CHARACTERS
- ADULT FEMALE -

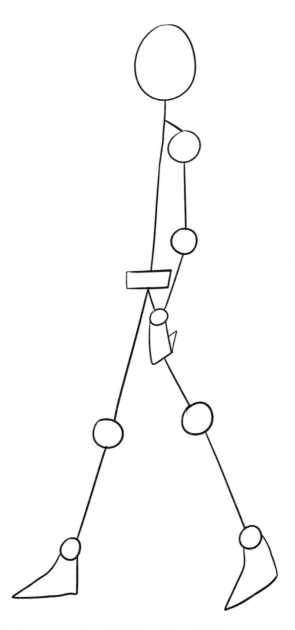

The first step will also start with the basic framework of the body and a pose of the character.

For a variation, we will draw the character facing sideways. When drawing a full body sidewards, only one side of the body is seen, that is why you only draw one arm and leg. But in this case, the character is in a dynamic pose which shows walking, that is why the other leg is shown. This gives the illusion that the character is taking steps.

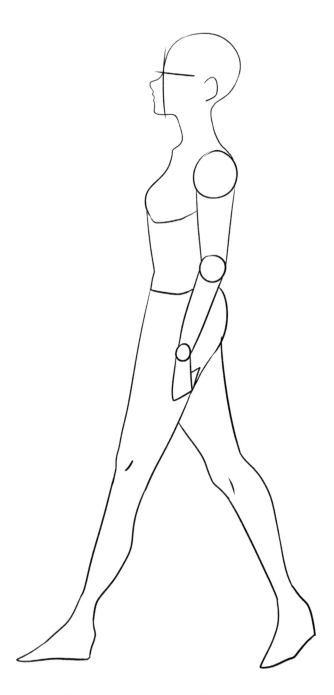

Like the first tutorials, outline the shape of the body to have a concrete idea of where to draw the body parts. Remember that arms and legs are drawn smoothly with rounded edges and not with sharp angles.

Draw the basic facial features of the character. Remember the basic tutorial when drawing faces that are in side view. The nose is more detailed and there is an outline for the lips. Also remember to draw the ear, it is placed slightly below the eyes.

Make sure to keep the lines smooth and a bit rounded to make her features softer and more feminine. A beauty mark was added below her eye to add a detail to her face. Feel free to add various facial details such as scars, freckles, or even blemishes!

Add the hairstyle of your choice. In this example, an elegant hair style suits the character very well. Make sure to add a variation of line width to add "volume" to the hair.

Don't be afraid to try and experiment in drawing hairstyles. As shown above, her hair is braided and curled to suggest femininity.

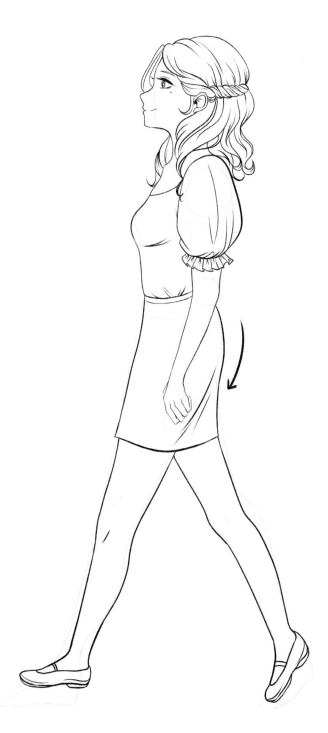

And of course, draw the clothes that will complement the character's features. Since we are going for a more elegant and soft character, a nice top with some details of ruffles and a skirt suits her well.

Be mindful of the folds of the clothes in dynamic poses like this. Since she is shown to be taking steps, the stress is on her leg, that is why the folds of her skirt follow the leg.

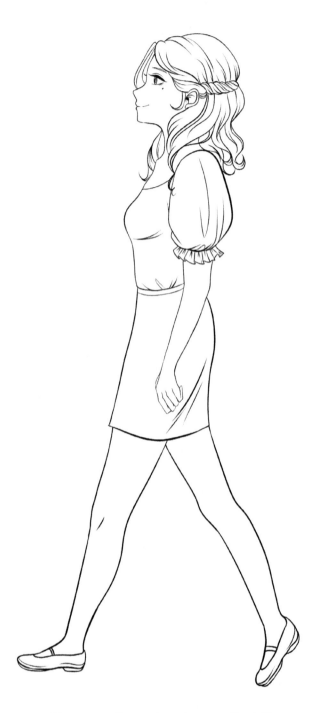

And now you're done with your female character! Remember that your choices are endless! There are a lot of personalities and unique designs you can incorporate in your character!

Picking out the right facial features, hair style, expressions, and clothes will complement each other and make it seem that your character really is alive!

DRAWING BASIC CHARACTERS
- ADULT MALE -

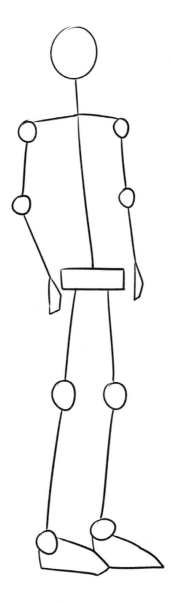

The first step will also start with the basic framework of the body and a pose of the character.

This is another sideview pose, but this time, the body will be facing slightly more frontwards while the head faces sideways.

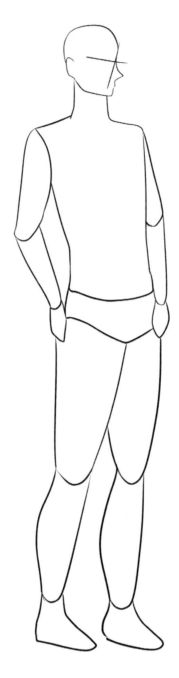

Like the first tutorials, outline the shape of the body to have a concrete idea of where to draw the body parts. Remember that arms and legs are drawn smoothly with rounded edges and not with sharp angles.

Draw the basic facial features of the character. Remember the basic tutorial when drawing faces that are in side view. The nose is more detailed and there is an outline for the lips. Also remember to draw the ear, it is placed slightly below the eyes.

Also add in the hair of the character to complete the whole head.

Draw the clothes you prefer. In this example, an outer wear was draw as an added clothing piece. Remember that in drawing clothes like jackets, cardigans, and coats, it should like as if it was "covering up" the upper body of the character, meaning it should not look like it's fitted like a glove.

Add the remaining clothing pieces such as the bottoms and the shoes of your characters. If you want, you can add some extra designs to your clothing pieces to make them less plain to make your drawing more interesting. You can start with simple designs such as stripes, like in this sample.

And now you're done with your male character! Remember that your choices in designing are endless! There are a lot of personalities and unique designs you can incorporate in your character!

Picking out the right facial features, hair style, expressions, and clothes will complement each other and make it seem that your character is really alive!

DRAWING AN ANIME GIRL WITH NEKOMIMI
- CAT EARS -

Start with a simple sketch of what pose you want to work with. Drawing a basic "stick man" can help a lot! Use shapes to define the body of the character. It is important to note that the body is more circular in certain parts and not just a big, flat rectangle.

After sketching out the body, we can proceed in drawing the clothes and hair. In this example, a traditional Japanese uniform was used. Draw some folds around the areas where there is movement so that the figure won't look flat and lifeless. In drawing hair and clothes, we must remember how gravity works. Make it more realistic by having them look draped across the figure.

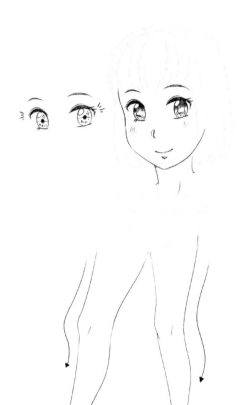

We can now proceed in lining the character to life! Starting with the face, draw the sketch cleanly using smooth lines. The eyes are one of the most important parts in drawing characters, so make sure to experiment on how you draw them! You can use various shapes to make it more unique.

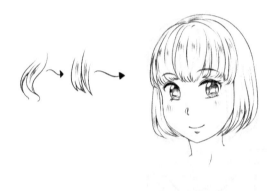

Also remember to draw legs and arms with curves. Human limbs are not straight! Drawing a slender form can make it look less stiff and unnatural.

In drawing the hair, make sure to not over-line the strands, try drawing it in "clumps" or sections, and add simple details.

Line all the clothing you sketched. Make sure to remember the folds of the clothes!

Add the additional accessories or body parts. In this case, nekomimi or cat ears! Draw them on top of the character's head.

Finalize the drawing by adding some shadings on the areas wherein there should be shadows, usually they are on the folds of the clothes and around the edges of the face and arms.

And you're done!

DRAWING CHARACTERS WITH MINIMAL BACKGROUND

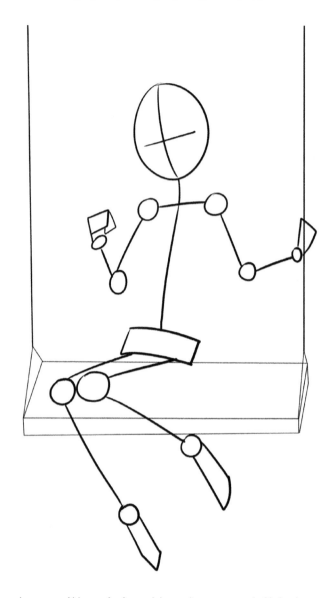

For drawing characters with minimal background, it is important to think about the ambiance or the overall feel of the drawing. Like incorporating specific expressions, poses, and clothing for your character, the ambiance will also add to the personality of the character.

In this example, we will draw a peaceful ambiance by adding a simple background and of course a character design that matches it.

Always start with the platform on which the character would be sitting and the framework of the character.

Like the other tutorials, proceed in drawing the head of the character which includes the face, eyes, nose, brows, mouth and the hair. As always, incorporate the personality and now think about the ambiance of the drawing.

Since we want to achieve a peaceful illustration, drawing the character with a serene expression will suit the ambiance well. Having the character frown will contradict the feel of the drawing and the character would look out of place.

The next step is to draw the clothes of the character.

The character is sitting down and the clothing is loose, and since it is a gown, the volume of the fabric is bigger compared to casual clothings. In this case, the folds of the gown are more visible and they look flowing especially from down the knees since the fabric would be "hanging" by that area.

Add additional details that will help in making the character look appropriate for the ambiance that you chose. Since we want to have a peaceful looking drawing, a pair of angel wings and halo would complete the character's look.

The last part would be adding the background details. Simple details can add big impact to the drawing.

In this example, the swing would be hanging from a tree, and that is why some parts of the tree can be drawn as well as some falling leaves.

Notice how small details gave the illustration a better feel to it. It made the drawing look more alive as well.

And now the drawing is done! The ambiance of a drawing can easily be defined with the character's pose, expression, and the minimal background details.

When drawing other themes, it is important to think about what feeling you are going for. Would you like the drawing to be romantic? Scary? Or even sad? If you are already set with what ambiance you want, the additional details will come along easier.

ANIME CHARACTER TROPES:
MAGICAL GIRL

One of the most common anime character trope is the magical girl. Usually, young girls are given magical powers to fight off evil and protect the people, common themes that are present are friendship and young love.

Magical girls usually fight in an ensemble. The group of magical girls would have a theme wherein each member would be assigned of a particular identity. For example, one group would have elemental powers, so one would have water powers, the others air, fire earth, etc.

Drawing magical girls would follow the basic rules in drawing characters. Starting off with a pose that defines their personality, followed by the fundamental features such as the face and body, clothing, and hair style.

The key point in drawing magical girls is to show their youth and emphasize which theme you have chosen for them. Like in the example above, her theme is heavy on flowers and ribbons. You can have various themes for your magical girl character, but make sure to show it through their clothing and accessories!

ANIME CHARACTER TROPES:
MAID

Another common anime character trope is the maid (butler if the character is masculine). Maid characters usually serve their masters diligently.

The most recognizable "feature" of maid characters would be their impractical outfits, since in manga, almost characters are usually heavily exaggerated; maid outfits are tacky clothing wherein the dresses and aprons are decorated with frills and laces. This is often used to show the wealth and tastes of the masters they are serving.

Drawing maids would follow the basic rules in drawing characters. Starting off with a pose that defines their personality, followed by the fundamental features such as the face and body, clothing, and hair style.

The key point in drawing maids is drawing their uniform accordingly. maids usually wear a dress underneath their aprons. The style and design varies and would depend on your preferences. You can make it as simple as it can be or as frilly like the example above! Butlers usually wear tailored suits to match the maids.

ANIME CHARACTER TROPES:
NINJA

A common anime character trope is the ninja. Ninjas are trained agents that were present as early as 15th century Japan. Ninjas are warriors that serve their masters for various activities which includes espionage, deception, and assassination.

Ninjas are known to be swift and deadly. They were trained to not make any sound during missions and to accomplish their objectives no matter what. They are also famous for their ability of camouflage and disguises.

Drawing ninjas would follow the basic rules in drawing characters. Starting off with a pose that defines their personality, followed by the fundamental features such as the face and body, clothing, and hair style.

The key point in drawing ninjas is to show their outfits well. In the example above, the ninja outfit was already modified according to personal preferences, but traditional ninja outfits are usually all-black and hide the head and half the face.

You can always consult references to see how traditional ninja outfits look like, but variation can always be added. They also carry various weapons for their missions such as but not limited to darts, katana, spikes, and poison.

ANIME CHARACTER TROPES:
PIRATE

A common anime character trope is the pirate. Pirates are popular characters among various forms of media, including anime. They have the same stereotypes like pirates from televisions and movies, tough and resourceful. They sail the oceans for the most valuable treasures in land and sea.

Pirates in anime are portrayed similarly like pirates in other media, their designs usually include eye patches, tricornes (hat), coats, boots, and some form of weaponry.

Drawing pirates would follow the basic rules in drawing characters. Starting off with a pose that defines their personality, followed by the fundamental features such as the face and body, clothing, and hair style.

The key point in drawing pirates is to draw their outfits accurately. Pirates are typically seen to be wearing eye patches, high boots, and coats. They also carry jewelry (from their loots!), and weapons for fighting (usually either swords or guns).

DRAWING TWO CHARACTERS

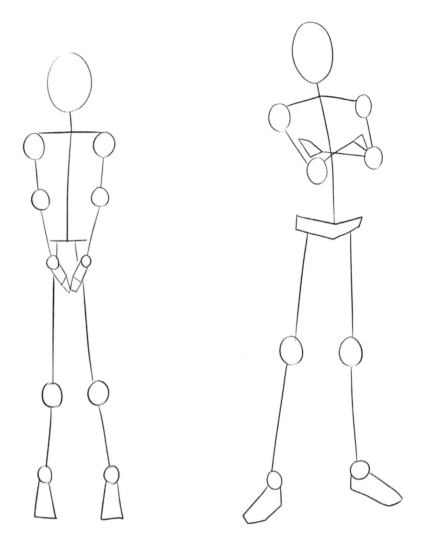

Drawing two characters is pretty easy. Like the first drawing tutorials, we usually start by drawing the frameworks of the body. But, an important thing to remember when drawing multiple bodies is to think about any differences between them.

Say for example, the other is a feminine character and the other one is masculine, it is expected that the feminine character would be shorter and more slender as compared to the other one.

This also includes their height; you need to take note if there is any height differences between the two characters you are going to draw. Finally, always make sure to observe the proportion even if there are differences between the two characters.

It is easier to draw when the characters are just standing side by side. But it is a different story if the characters are interacting closely with each other.

When the characters are just standing close to each other, you can draw either of the them first, but say for example they are in a more dynamic and complicated pose like the example above, the drawing process may be a bit different from a standard pose.

In the example above, one character is held up by the other. Even if the pose is dynamic, always apply proper proportions for both. It also smart to start with the character which is holding up the other one since it will be like the "base" of the other character.

Various poses will have a different technique of which character to draw first. Think about which will make the process easier.

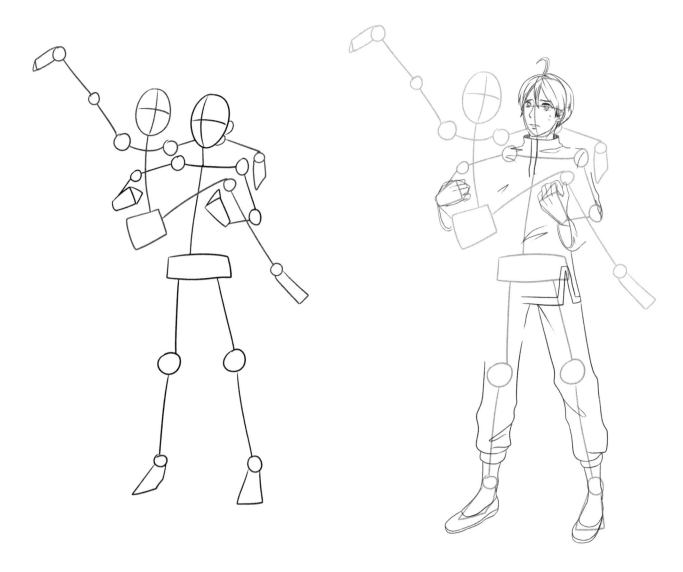

The next steps would be to draw the first character. First draw the head and its facial features, then the clothes, and the rest of the body parts. Remember that there would be another character that would be drawn beside him so make sure to leave out some spaces for the other character.

It is also important to be mindful of how will you make the characters look like they are interacting with one another. One thing to consider is their eye contact and their facial expressions.

Draw the second character with the same steps starting from the head and the facial features to the clothes and body parts. Remember to make the two characters interact.

In this example, even if they are not looking at each other, you can tell what emotions the two have. The one who is holding the other one has a tired expression while the one being held up is cheerful and unaware of the other's worry.

And now you're done! In drawing multiple characters together, it is important to show their interaction if you would be drawing them in dynamic poses. Simple expressions and the way they are posed can already tell a story between your characters!

Like in this example, you can tell that the girl being held up is someone who is cheerful and carefree, while the guy carrying her is a bit troubled or worried. You can even think that they are like close friends or even something more!

Drawing characters in various scenarios can help in showing their personalities, relationship, and even their stories!

FRAMING CHARACTERS

"FRAME"

Framing is a technique used in various forms of art wherein only specific subjects are seen inside a "frame". When subjects are framed, there is mostly "blocking, wherein the closest subject in the viewer's perspective blocks some parts of the objects behind. This technique is used to create focus as well as dimension in a piece of art whether it is illustration or photography.

Framing is also frequently used when drawing manga, aside from having focus on specific characters or subjects, it also makes the drawing alive in the sense that the subjects are arranged in a composite form.

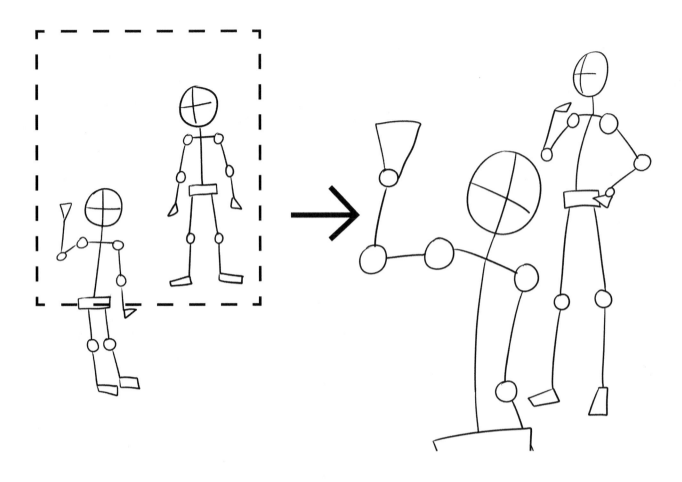

In framing characters, you start by thinking of which character you want to put "in front" or the closest to your perspective.

In the example above, we can see that one of the characters is drawn as the main focus while another is at the background as a supporting subject. Think of it as shooting a photo, one person can be nearer the camera while the others may be farther away.

Now that the frameworks of the characters are positioned, we can start drawing the characters themselves! Like the tutorial in drawing multiple characters, it would be easier to draw one full character first rather than switching between them.

In this example, it can make drawing easier to draw the character in focus then proceed to the character in the background.

Draw the first character starting with the head, facial features, clothes and the body parts. Drawing the character in focus will make it easier later on since the nearest character would be blocking some or most of the background characters' features depending on their poses.

In the example, the character in focus will block some part of the background character's clothes and arm parts.

Proceed with the background character's features as well. Keep in mind of their facial expressions and poses. Even if the characters are not directly interacting, the illustration must feel unified.

In the example above, the focus subject is waving in front, his eyes are looking forward. The background character is also looking forward as if both characters are looking at the same thing or person.

And now you're done! You can use this technique to create more dimensions and make the illustration more alive. You can also make variations with the poses, the number of characters inside the frame, and even the angle to create livelier drawings!

DRAWING CHARACTERS ON ITEMS

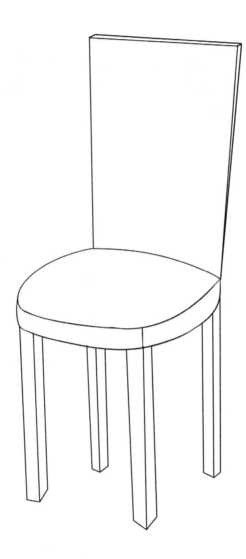

In this tutorial, we will draw a character with an object, but instead of holding it, the character will be on it. Usually characters would be sitting, laying, on something like a chair or table, or any platform.

Like the tutorial with holding objects, it would be easier to start in drawing the object before the character itself. For this example, we will draw a character sitting on a chair.

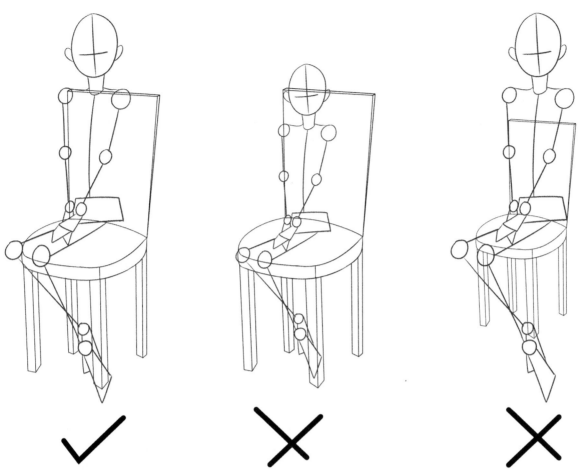

The next step will be drawing the framework of the body on the chair itself. Since we drew the chair first, it will be easier to draw the body of the character that matches the size of the chair! Be mindful of making the body too small or too big for the object.

Continue drawing the character by adding the facial features like the eyes, nose, mouth, brows, and even the hair.

Always remember to incorporate your desired expression and the personality of the character in their facial features.

The next step is to draw the clothes of the character.

Since the character is sitting down, try to imagine how the folds of the clothing will look like. Depending on what clothing the character is wearing, some will have more folds than the others. In this example, the character is wearing a short, pleated skirt, that is why the folds are very visible. If the character is wearing something very fitted, then it should follow that there are less folds.

And now the character is done! Take note of how the ratio of the character is proportional to the size of the chair.

The same rules apply whether the object the character on is a bed or a bench, make sure that the size of the platform suits the size of the character, unless, you are drawing a really big chair or bed, then of course make it bigger than the character.

DRAWING CHARACTERS WITH ITEMS

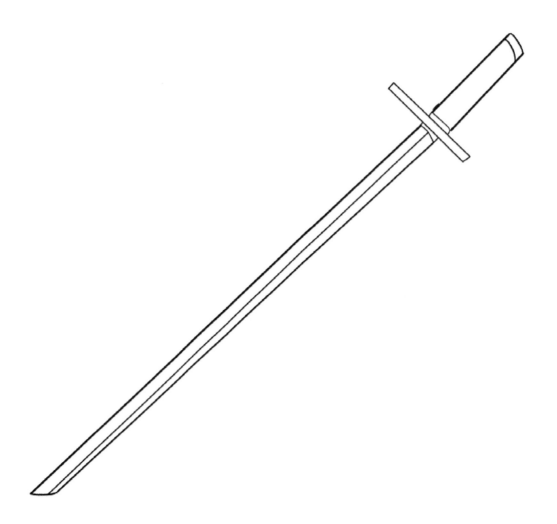

Start by thinking of what object do you want your character to hold, it can be anything like house objects, weapons, or food.

In this example, we will use a sword since the character is a prince. It would be smart to look up different kinds and designs for objects like weapons.

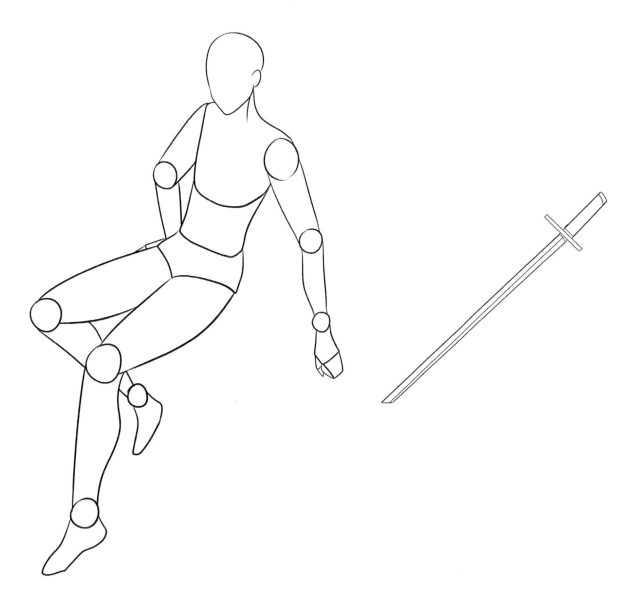

The next step will be drawing the framework of the body which will show the desired pose.

Since the character would be holding a specific item, make sure to have the hands positioned accordingly. In this example, the character would be holding the sword in one hand in a casual and relaxed pose.

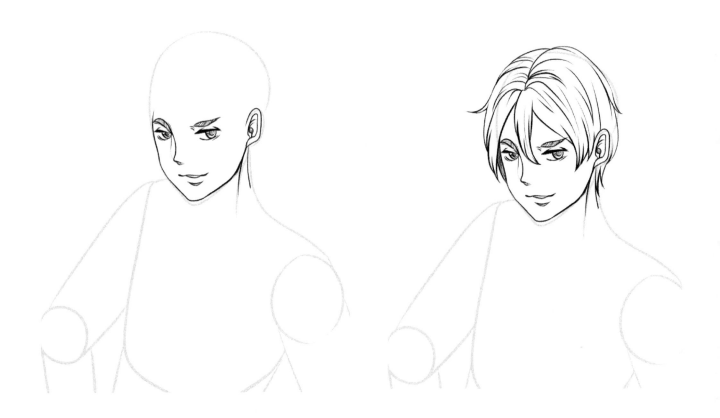

Continue drawing the character by adding the facial features like the eyes, nose, mouth, brows, and even the hair.

Always remember to incorporate your desired expression and the personality of the character in their facial features.

The next step is to draw the clothes of the character. Since in this example, we are drawing a prince influenced by the western culture, we will draw his elegant suit with matching boots.

Draw the object to be held by the character. An important thing to remember when drawing objects is to make sure that the size of the object is proportional to the character.

Keep in mind the object's ratio to the size of your character. In this example, the character is an adult male, that is why the sword held is just right for him.

If the character would have been shorter, then the sword should be drawn smaller to match the size of the character.

Drawing anime is never easy, like any other styles of illustration; consistent practice and motivation is needed to improve further. Making better illustrations is usually the combination of your own preferences in terms of character definition and the most basic principles in figure drawing.

But at the same time, never be afraid of making mistakes in your drawing! Always finish the illustrations that you have started, and don't give up halfway when you notice that something is off with it since it will be easier to know on what parts to improve if you can see the whole picture. Evaluating the mistakes in your drawing means that you have to revisit all the things that you have learned before; from the body and face proportions, the shapes, and even the details. After knowing your mistakes, have time to redraw your illustration and keep in mind the things that you thinkare needed to be improved.

Drawing anime is never easy. Like any other styles of illustration, consistent practice and motivation is needed to keep improving. Making better illustrations is usually the combination of developing your own unique styles and preferences in terms of character definition and mastering the most basic principles in figure drawing.

Never be afraid of making mistakes in your drawings! Always finish the illustrations that you have started, and don't give up halfway when you notice that something is off with it since it will be easier to know on what parts to improve when you can see the whole picture. Evaluating the mistakes in your drawings means that you have to revisit all the things that you have learned before; from the body and face proportions, the shapes, and even the details. After knowing your mistakes, have time to redraw your illustration and keep in mind the things that you think need to be improved.

And remember - being good at something does not happen overnight! Instead of pressuring yourself to create something that is perfect, focus on the parts where you are good and improve on the parts where you are not that good.

Are you good at drawing hair? That's good! Explore more materials and inspiration to have a wide variation in your drawings! Not very good in drawing clothing? That's okay! Make some time to browse through your favorite fashion magazines and the internet to find some really good references.

Remember that even the greatest painters used to observe still life and apply it to their artworks.

Happy drawing!

Thank you for getting our book!

If you enjoy using it and you found it useful in your journey
of learning to draw, we would greatly appreciate
your review on Amazon.

Just head on over to this book's Amazon page and click
"Write a customer review".

We read each and every one of them. Thanks!

Printed in Great Britain
by Amazon